Learning More About My Feelings

Carmen Jimenez-Pride
MSW, LCSW, LISW-CP, SAP, RYT, RCYT, RPT-S

Focus on Feelings®: Learning More About My Feelings

Copyright © 2021 Carmen Jimenez-Pride
All rights reserved.

Focus on Feelings® is a trademarked and copyrighted brand.

eBook: 978-1-7344557-7-9
Hardcover: 978-1-7344557-6-2
Soft Cover: 978-1-7344557-8-6
Library of Congress Control Number: 2020952850

This book may not be reproduced, relabeled or used in any commercial manner whatsoever without the written permission of the creator.

For permission request please contact the author directly at:

Carmen Jimenez-Pride
www.carmenpride.com
Carmen@outspokenllc.com

Carmen Jimenez-Pride, LCSW, RPT-S

ABOUT THE AUTHOR

Carmen Jimenez-Pride, creator of Focus on Feelings® is a License Clinical Social Worker and Registered Play Therapist Supervisor, Certified EMDR Therapist, Internal Family Systems Therapist. She is an international speaker, award winning best-selling author and business consultant.

Carmen Jimenez-Pride is also the founder of Diversity in Play Therapy Inc. and the host of the Diversity in Play Therapy Summit.

Contact: **www.carmenpride.com**

Email: **Carmen@outspokenllc.com**

CONFIDENT

CONFIDENT

Confident means being sure of one's self or trusting in one's abilities which makes one feel very bold especially around others.

On Monday, Alex's teacher gave the class their new spelling words. Alex studied every day for his spelling test on Friday. Alex woke up on Friday morning and his mother asked him if he was ready for his test. Alex said "Yes! I'm ready. I feel confident that I know all the words".

CURIOUS

CURIOUS

To be curious means to be excited, and ready to know and learn new things. It also means asking questions, investigating, and exploring. We can be curious about things we do not understand and have questions about things that don't have easy answers. We are curious to learn about new, and important people.

𝒜manda always wondered why there was such a great distance between the sky and the earth. Every morning, she would stand under the sun and stare at the sky, she was curious about how far the sky was from the earth.

IRRITATED

IRRITATED

To be irritated means getting upset, impatient or uncomfortable easily. We can feel irritated when other people we don't like are around us, or when people say things that annoy us. We can also be irritated when things do not go as we planned.

Marcus apologized to his friends for yelling at them during the soccer game on Thursday. "Please forgive me. I was only irritated that I could not make a goal. I was also irritated because the coach would not tell the players to pass me the ball.

IGNORED

IGNORED

To be ignored means being deliberately avoided and neglected by someone. This happens when they pretend not to notice us or see us.

Justin felt ignored by his friends at school because they wouldn't sit with him at lunch or include him in their weekend.

BORED

BORED

To be bored means to feel you have nothing to do. This happens when we lose interest in everything.

Chris is tired of being in the house and playing alone. Chris is bored with playing the same games without his friends.

PROUD

PROUD

To be proud means to feel honored, satisfied or happy about an accomplishment.

*R*eggie received his report card and reviewed his grades. He worked hard in his math class and remembered to turn in all his homework. When he felt proud to see an "A" beside his math grade. His hard work paid off, he felt Proud.

CONFUSED

CONFUSED

A feeling of not being able to think clearly or understand. feeling puzzled about something.

Jessica had a hard time making friends at her new school because she couldn't speak or understand Spanish, and most of the kids didn't understand English. She always felt confused whenever they spoke Spanish to her.

CALM

CALM

To be calm means to feel peace and quiet, especially from anger and anxiety. To breathe easy and relax.

For several weeks Kia worked hard on her science fair project. The morning she had to take her project to school her father said "Kia, I can't be there, but I know you will be amazing. You have worked really hard". She smiled and felt really calm about entering her science project in the science fair.

DISAPPOINTED

DISAPPOINTED

To be disappointed means feeling sad or frustrated when a strongly desired expectation is not met; or when you don't get what you want.

Sophia's dad promised to buy her a new toy on her birthday. But he failed to do so. Sophia felt very disappointed because she had really hoped for a new toy to show to her friends.

HURT

HURT

To feel pain when we're injured or to feel unhappy when people treat us badly. Being treated badly results in feelings being hurt.

Lincoln wouldn't speak a word to his older brother. He felt hurt that John would eat all the muffins and leave none for him.

UGH

UGH

We say 'Ugh,' when we want to express disgust or annoyance. So if you don't like something and you don't have a perfect way to say it, you can say 'Ugh!'

"Ugh! I don't want to do my notes" said Sheri. I would rather be playing a video game or watching TV.

JEALOUS

JEALOUS

To be jealous means to feel displeasure or troubled by worries that one might have been replaced in someone's affection. Feeling like a friend likes someone else may cause feelings of jealousy.

"Why wouldn't Samantha say hi to me today?" Rebecca wondered. Rebecca noticed that her best friend, Samantha, had been avoiding her the whole day. Samantha was feeling jealous because Rebecca was spending more time with the new girl at school.

OVERWHELMED

OVERWHELMED

To be overwhelmed means to be overpowered by our feelings, and emotions. It could be the feeling of extreme excitement, sadness, or surprise.

Caleb was overwhelmed with happiness when he saw the number of children that had shown up for his birthday party. He'd been worried that no one would come because he was the newest kid in school.

SHY

SHY

To be shy means to be reserved and disinclined to familiar approach. To avoid talking to, or looking directly at others.

Evelyn felt shy when she was called to say her speech to the class. Evelyn always felt shy when she had to stand in front of her class and speak. She usually stared at her feet while she talked.

HOPELESS

HOPELESS

To be hopeless means to lose trust or hope and be in despair. It also means not expecting anything positive. We can feel hopeless when we are disappointed by people, or when the things we want do not come to us. Or when there is no way to solve a problem that greatly bothers us.

Ciera felt hopeless as she walked around the entire forest without finding a way out. She felt trapped in the magical forest, and her friends weren't making things easier.
"We can never find our way out of here. Nobody comes out of the magical forest. We are trapped forever!" They cried, all feeling hopeless.

FOCUSED

FOCUSED

Directing all of one's efforts towards achieving a particular goal. Extreme concentration on a task.

Margie's science teacher told the class "If you're focused while in class, completing your homework may be easier". Margie worked hard to remain focused in class.

BRAVE

BRAVE

To be brave means to be strong and keep going in the face of fear.

𝓐lthough Nathan was nervous playing golf against players that had played longer. He chose to be brave and not give up. In the end, he came in first place.

CHILL

CHILL

Without anxiety about things. Feeling relaxed, calm, relieved of aggravation. To be in a state of calmness and remain relaxed without a focused task.

Ten more minutes until the last bell of school the school year. Katrina worked hard all year long and how she is able to chill for the summer. She is looking forward to chilling by the pool with friends for the summer break.

PLAYFUL

PLAYFUL

Liking to play, always eager to play, and enjoy. To be playful could also mean being funny, joking, or joyous.

When Cory feels good, he is playful with his friends. He enjoys telling jokes and making everyone laugh.

REJECTED

To be rejected means to feel unwanted or neglected when people refuse to accept us or what we have to offer.

Maxwell felt rejected, the other kids didn't want to include him because he didn't want to act or be like them. He felt rejected for who he was.

CPSIA information can be obtained
at www.ICGtesting.com
Printed in the USA
LVHW070908050421
683454LV00002B/2